Bug
Faces

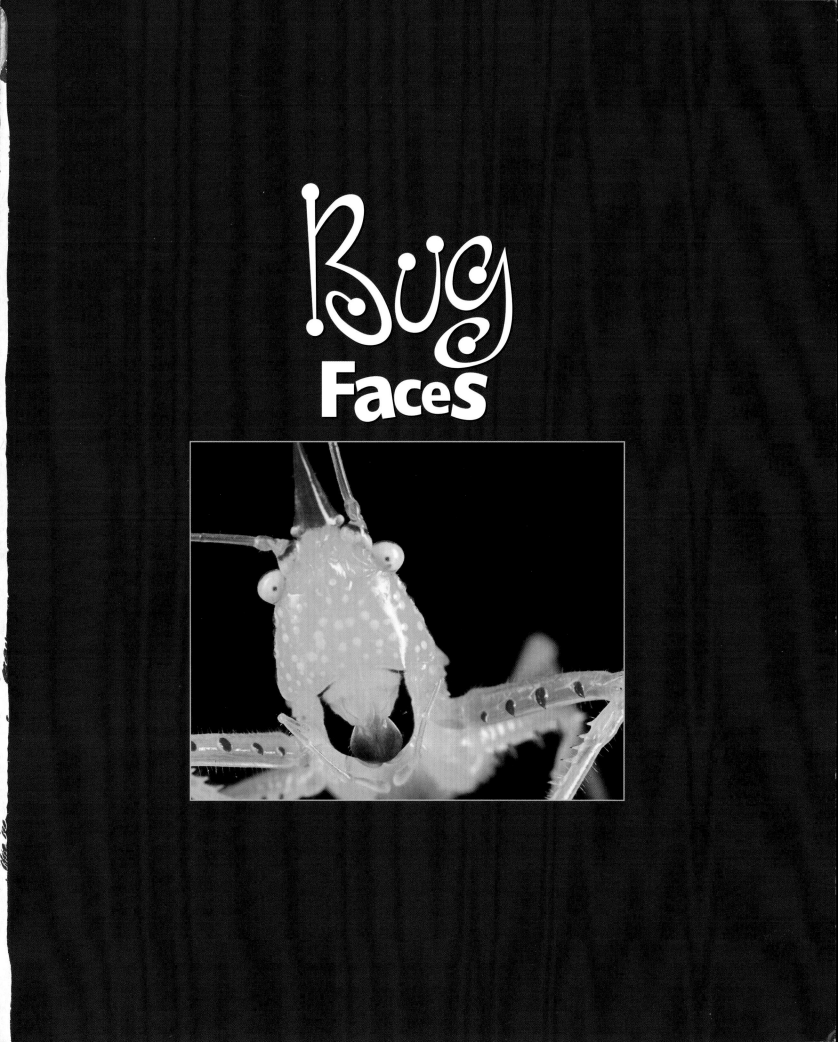

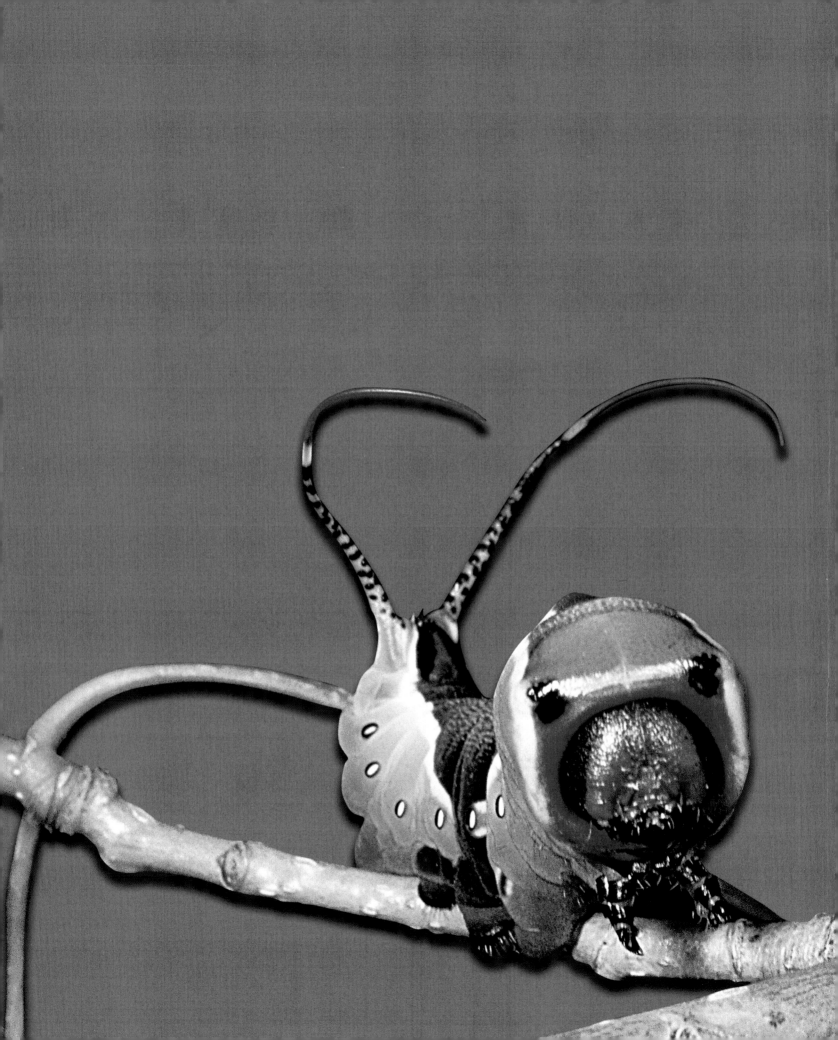

Bug Faces

by Darlyne A. Murawski

□ NATIONAL GEOGRAPHIC SOCIETY

Washington, D.C.

Introduction

Chances are you've seen a bug today. Maybe it was a fly or a spider or a caterpillar. A scientist would tell you that a true bug is a certain kind of insect. But to most people, a bug is anything small that creeps, crawls, or flies. That's why in this book you'll meet lots of different kinds of insects plus a couple of their relatives: the spider and the daddy-longlegs.

A bug's face is quite different from a person's. Take eyes, for example. Some bugs, like the dragonfly, have huge, bulging eyes that take up most of the face. Others have eyes arranged neatly in rows or in the shape of a triangle.

Their mouths are designed for sucking or chewing. Those that suck have a hollow tube that they use like a straw. Those that chew have strong jaws for grinding and feelers that pretaste food. Bugs "smell" with their antennae. Some bugs even have false faces that they flash to startle an attacker. Read on and discover for yourself the amazing variety of bug faces.

DRAGONFLY

This **DEER FLY** looks like it has green-and-red eyes. That's because light is being reflected from thousands of tiny eyes that make up the two large compound eyes. Each tiny eye is sensitive to movement. No wonder it's hard to swat a fly! The deer fly likes to drink blood. Its stubby red antennae help guide it to warm bodies. Razor-sharp mouthparts slice open the skin, and spongelike pads mop up the blood. This fly is especially fond of deer, but other animals will do — even people!

Big-Eyed

BLO

ODSUCKER

Earth to Mars

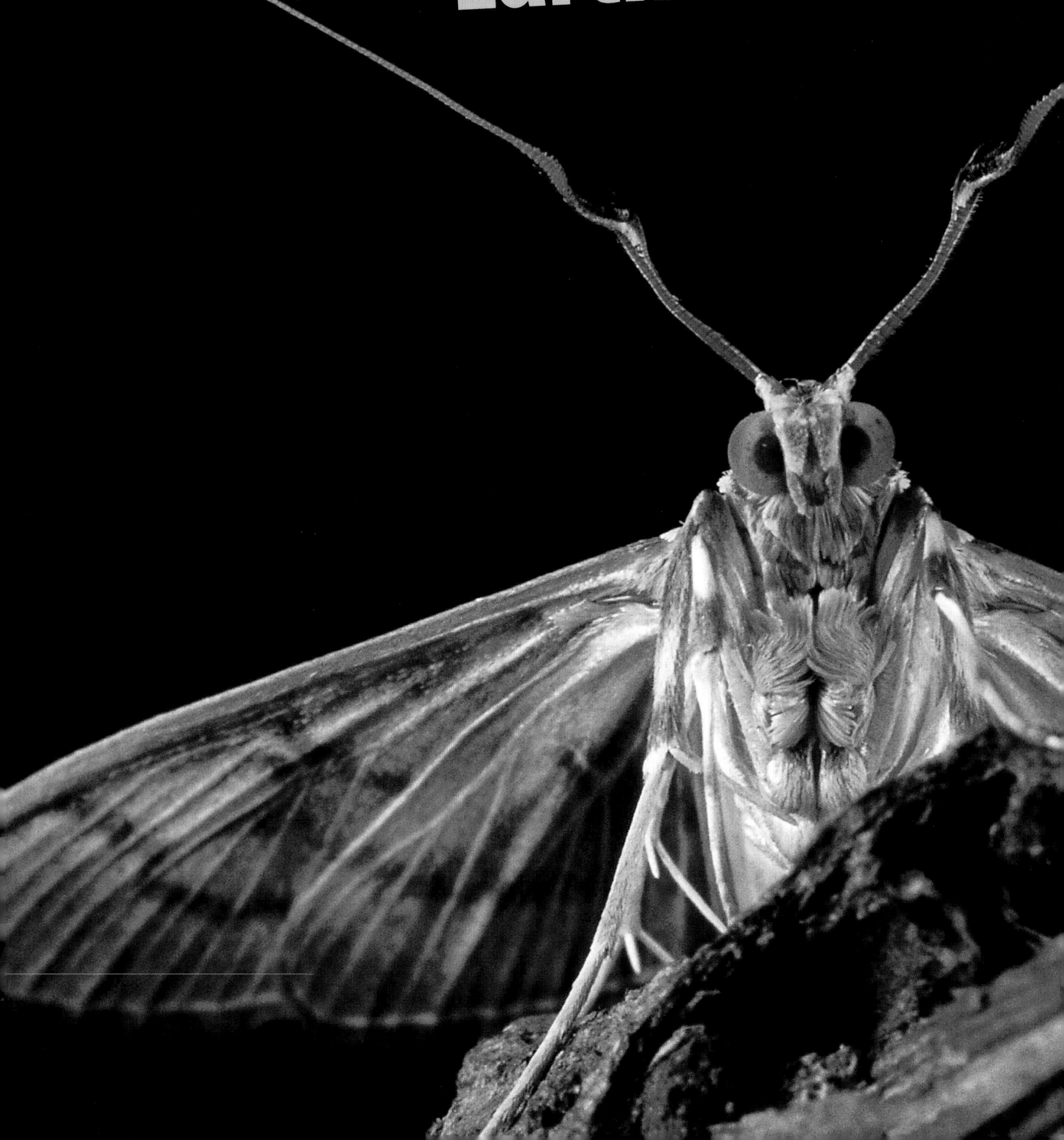

The
SNOUT MOTH
has notched, wirelike
antennae.
Many moths have
feathery antennae.
None have club-tipped
ones like butterflies do.
Antennae pick up signals from
the air. They detect smells that
help the moth find a mate. They also
help sense air speed. This moth can
use the two feelers in the middle of its
face like windshield wipers to clean its
eyes. This moth is not really cross-eyed.
Those dark circles are reflected light.
Most moths are active at night. Unlike
butterflies, moths rest with their wings open.

A busy **BUMBLEBEE** lands on a flower and unfolds a long tube called a proboscis from beneath its head. It uses the tube like a straw to sip nectar. Fuzzy yellow hairs on the head collect grains of pollen that the bee carries from flower to flower. The jointed rods on either side of the drinking tube are antennae. They act like a nose and tell the bee when it's found something s w e e t to eat.

HUNTING
hidden treasure

FOR

Where's the FACE?

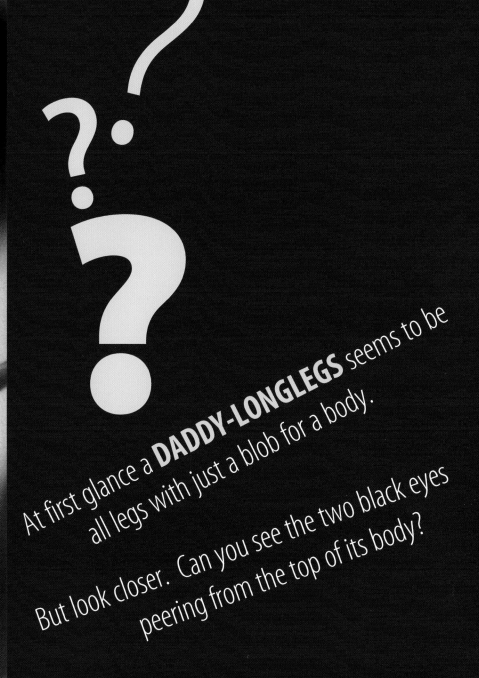

At first glance a **DADDY-LONGLEGS** seems to be all legs with just a blob for a body.

But look closer. Can you see the two black eyes peering from the top of its body?

Between the front legs are its big jaws. But don't worry. It won't bite you. Daddy-longlegs like to eat insects and nibble on mushrooms. Watch out, though. Some give off a stinky smell when disturbed. Although it has eight legs, it is not a spider.

FOR CRYING

OUT LO

OUD

This wide-eyed, hairy monster is a **CICADA**. It's one of nature's noisiest insects.

In summer, groups of males sit in treetops and call for their mates.

What looks like a speaker box in the middle of the face has nothing to do with sound. It is part of the cicada's feeding system. Inside is a powerful muscle attached to a pump. When the cicada sticks its stout proboscis into a branch, the pump pulls sap out of the tree into the cicada.

JUNGLE

GIA

You'd have to travel to a rain forest to run into this giant three-inch-long **COCKROACH**. Smaller varieties live everywhere except Earth's coldest places. Those black patches that resemble headphones are compound eyes that can see in all directions. The long feelers near its mouth are called palps. They pretaste food and keep this critter from eating something harmful. Did you know cockroaches have been around more than 300 million years!

LEAN,

eating machine

GRASSHOPPERS

are plant-eaters that can
cause major damage to crops.
They don't have teeth, but they do
have strong jaws for grinding food.
In addition to their big compound eyes they
have three simple eyes that form a triangle between
their antennae. These eyes are sensitive to light.
They tell the grasshopper when its time to eat
and when it's time to rest.

GREEN

Here's Looking at YOU, YOU, & YOU...

Like other spiders, the **NURSERY-WEB SPIDER** has only simple eyes. Each of the eight eyes has one lens. Together they help the spider see in several directions at once — all the better to hunt down its dinner. Just below the two rows of eyes are powerful jaws covered with sensitive hairs. The jaws are tipped with sharp fangs that inject poison into prey. Female nursery-webs use their jaws to cradle their young in a huge egg sac.

SEEING SPOTS?

The **LADYBUG** looks like it's wearing a white helmet and sunglasses. The helmet is really part of the skeleton that protects the beetle's head. The dark glasses are compound eyes. Hairs on the upper lip help it find its favorite food: tiny, soft-bodied pests called aphids that damage roses and other plants. It uses its chewing mouthparts to eat as many as a hundred aphids a day! Whether you call it a ladybug, a lady beetle, or a ladybird beetle, just remember: There are male ladybugs, too!

Ouch! A mother **MOSQUITO** uses needle-like jaws to pierce your skin, then she sucks your blood through a tube. What looks like a leg behind the tube is really her lower lip. It helps steady the tube to keep it on target. Her antennae are sensitive to temperature and help guide her to your warm body. Only female mosquitoes drink blood. They need it to develop their eggs. Males *and* females use their long feeding tubes to sip nectar from flowers.

Fill 'er Up

Long-Faced & Blue

A **WEEVIL** is a beetle with a stretched-out head that looks like a snout. That's why weevils are sometimes called snout beetles. Not all weevils are blue like this one from New Guinea, but they all feed on plants. They use the chewing mouthparts at the end of the snout to drill into the fruit and seeds they eat. Females lay eggs at the end of these holes.

In some weevils the club-tipped antennae fold into grooves on the snout.

Scientists have named about 60,000 kinds of weevils. Have you seen any?

sLuRRrp!

The **PAINTED LADY BUTTERFLY** uses its long proboscis like a soda straw to sip nectar from a flower.

Butterflies can't bite or chew. They can only drink liquids. A pump in the head draws the nectar into the body. When it's finished feeding, the butterfly rolls its proboscis into a neat coil. In some butterflies the proboscis is longer than the body! Did you know that butterflies taste with their feet and smell with their antennae? They are active during the day.

Many butterflies, moths, and their caterpillars use False

This moth flicks open its wings to expose two large false eyes called eyespots. An enemy might think twice before attacking.

To protect itself, this caterpillar bows its head and puffs up its back to reveal fake eyes complete with reflections.

FaceS

false faces to scare away birds and other predators.

Another caterpillar, from Central America, changes the shape of its head so it looks like a poisonous snake.

As a defense, this caterpillar inflates a facelike mask with a startling red border and spits acid from what looks like a smiley mouth !

For Luis Carlos and all young bug-lovers

Published by the National Geographic Society
1145 17th St. N.W.
Washington, D. C. 20036

Book design by Holli Rathman

The text is set in MyriaMM and Futura, with the title type in Treehouse.

The world's largest nonprofit scientific and educational
organization, the National Geographic Society was founded in
1888 "for the increase and diffusion of geographic knowledge."
Since then it has supported scientific exploration and spread
information to its more than nine million members worldwide.
The National Geographic Society educates and inspires millions
every day through magazines, books, television programs, videos,
maps and atlases, research grants, the National Geographic Bee,
teacher workshops, and innovative classroom materials.

The Society is supported through membership dues and
income from the sale of its educational products.
Call 1-800-NGS-LINE (647-5463) for more information.
Visit our Web site: www.nationalgeographic.com

Library of Congress Cataloging-in-Publication Data
Murawski, Darlyne A.
Bug faces / by Darlyne A. Murawski.
p.   cm.
Summary: Presents close-up photographs of insect faces and describes some of their
unique facial features, including compound eyes and pincher jaws.
ISBN 0-7922-7557-8 (hc)
1. Insects—Juvenile literature. 2. Arachnida—Juvenile literature. [1. Insects.] I. Title.
QL467.2 .M87 2000
595.7—dc21   00-028171

Printed in the U.S.A.

Front cover: Deer fly
Half-title page: Katydid
Title page: Puss moth caterpillar